CREATIVE WAYS TO BUILD YOUR FAMILY TEAM

PRACTICAL EVERYDAY TOOLS THAT WILL MAKE AN IMMEDIATE DIFFERENCE

KELSEY & JEREMY PRYOR

The Library of Congress Cataloging-in-Publication
Data is on file with the Library of Congress
ISBN-13: 978-0-578-52610-2

TO THOSE STARTING TO BUILD
THEIR TEAMS. MAY THESE 31
IDEAS JUMPSTART YOUR OWN
CREATIVITY AS YOU ESTABLISH
YOUR MULTIGENERATIONAL
FAMILY.

FOREWORD

Alyssa and I can single-handedly trace so much of our family culture, health, and vision directly to Jeremy and April. I can only count on one hand the number of people that have had such a noticeable effect on us (and I'm talking in business, discipleship, family, and every area of life). The Pryor's are one of those people.

Why? Well, for a few reasons. One, we've actively pursued them over the last six to seven years because there haven't been many other families we've wanted to emulate more than them. Two, mainly because I don't know many other families who are as intentional as they are.

They have thought through and tried to solve so many things and problems. Most of their unique skill of fresh, creative out of the box thinking, coupled with their level of dedication to building a family team, is unequivocally world class and has blessed so many.

What is really fun is the book you are now holding in your hands contains some of their most well worn, battle-tested, or just plain fun tools they've used over the years to really shape them into such a powerful family team.

Being a team doesn't come easy. It doesn't come naturally.

It needs vision, intention, leadership, and more.

But most of all it needs tools.

What we love about (and am somewhat jealous about!) this book, is this is some of the best ones that we heard and asked about over the years while staying at their house and on trips together. You get to hold it in your hands in one concise and practical place!

Even though these tools range from serious to funny, and can span or adapt to all ages, watch out because these tools can single-handedly begin to transform your family culture, your home, the sibling relationships, and the overall pulse and joy of your family team. I know that's what it did for us!

JEFF + ALYSSA BETHKE
authors of *31 Creative Ways To Love and Encourage Him & Her*

HOW TO GET THE MOST OUT OF THIS BOOK

Hey! We are so glad you picked up a copy of this book. In looking around the family landscape, we realized there was a lack of resources that were quick and easy to digest or that gave a wealth of help, tools, and battle-tested practices. So we decided to put together some of our favorite 'tools' for building a multi-generational team into one book. These are things we have done, adapted, changed, and have lived out in our own family.

Because there isn't quite another book like this one, here are a few things to note that we suggest or wanted to communicate that will give you the best experience possible as you dive in!

1. If you bought this book from our Family Teams store (shop. familyteams.com), that also means you have access to a corresponding video for each entry where Jeremy and April or one of their kids expands on the idea and brings it to life! If you bought the book on Amazon, you can find a link on our store (shop.familyteams.com) to purchase the videos!

2. While this could be done in 31 days, we'd suggest using it more like a manual where you flip around and focus in on one section at a time. If you need a helpful template, we recommend giving each entry about a week or two of focus. This is enough time to implement, experiment, iterate, then change or kick it into autopilot as a non-negotiable rhythm.

3. Please note that most of the ideas are appropriate for all ages of kids in the home (toddlers to teenagers), but there are a few that can practically apply only to one or two age groups. Because of that, we added some bonus ones to make sure there is plenty for everyone!

4. Remember this is a book of suggestions and ways we have tried to build our multi-generational team on mission over the years. This means we believe, encourage, and even prefer you use these 31 ways as starting points and something that catalyzes you to action. Feel free to adapt, change, or alter any of these to fit your family.

These tools are about freedom, fun, and implementing tools that actually work. So consider these ideas like a coaches playbook to get ideas, go back to the field, and give it your own unique spin.

TABLE OF CONTENTS

WAYS TO CONNECT:

These are tools designed to deepen the bonds between the team members in the family.

WAYS TO BE A TEAM:

These tools help the family work as a unit across age groups and various giftings to enjoy being together and accomplishing things as an integrated whole.

WAYS TO IMPROVE:

These tools help the household run more smoothly so you have the traction and energy to become a better team.

1

ONE ON ONES

WAYS TO CONNECT

We've done one on one's multiple ways, so before I dive into the "how" I'll say a bit about the "why."

My Dad was first introduced to this idea at the camp he, and later I, served at. There was a team of 20 teens enduring rigorous tasks, living in uncomfortable conditions and wrestling with deep spiritual issues for four weeks. The one on ones they had with the people serving together was crucial to their team spirit.

He came to the realization if they're so helpful to the team spirit of camp staff who are working hard, learning about the Lord and doing life together, doesn't that mean it could be equally beneficial for our Family Team? He wanted us, kids, to be used to starting those kinds of conversations with each other, about things we are going through, or finding commonalities, or merely having a directed light-hearted conversation. It's also crucial for them as parents to have heart-to-hearts regularly. There are some weeks where it's an hour long cry fest where we work through some tough issues. Some weeks they listen to our desires and try to make it happen (lessons we want to take, a person we want to see more often, an experience we want to have, etc.) and sometimes it's a simple update on things we've been feeling or thinking about.

So there are a few ways we have done it. Since there are seven of us, we try to do two each week. Initially, we did both of them back to back after our Sunday meeting. They lasted 30 minutes each. We have a mini-fridge stocked with fun drinks so we would get a fun drink and find a corner with our partner to chat. Since there's an odd amount of us, the first round of one on ones left one person without a partner so they would go off to write in their journal. Then for the second round of one on ones, Mom and Dad would team up to speak to the child that was journaling and talk to them about what they journaled, and the other kids would shuffle their partners.

That way sort of worked, but it made our Sunday meeting time much longer, and it was a bit much to do two back to back. The way we do it now is a bit more relaxed. Dad came up with a monthly schedule-"Week 1, Week 2, Week 3, Week 4." Each week has 2 columns-"Saturday and Sunday." So everyone has a one on one every Saturday and Sunday (except again, since there is an odd amount of us, one person has a "bi" each month). Everyone is in charge of initiating their own one on one. This also gives us more time to do something fun like go out for lunch or go see a movie because there's no specific start and stop time. I like to take Kaira rollerblading, Dad usually takes his partner out to lunch, and Mom often does her one on one around a puzzle.

It's totally up to you when and how you do your one on ones, but these are the ways we have tried and why we think they're important.

JOURNAL BELOW:

WRITE WHAT YOU LEARNED, HOW IT WENT, AND WHAT IMPACT IT'S HAVING ON YOUR FAMILY CULTURE.

2

KID ESSAYS

WAYS TO CONNECT

So this kind of goes with our first One on One idea. Dad mentioned how, since we have an odd number in the family, one person will go away and journal by themselves and then later bring their journal entry into a one on one with him and Mom.

You can do this whenever you want, it doesn't have to be based around One on Ones, and it doesn't have to be with both of you. I just like this idea because sometimes it's easier to process things by yourself in a journal and then talk about it later.

We journal by making a list of five things on our minds and then pick one to write a whole page about. We've talked through a lot of deep issues this way. This is how the "crush" conversation comes up sometimes, or we talk through a relational problem we're having with a friend, sibling, or even our parents. We find we discover something about the way we work or something we want to pursue.

We try to come away from that meeting with a solution to whatever it is we are thinking on. "Dad I feel like when I say "XYZ" you react "this way" and I don't like it." So we'll talk about how to change the way he reacts. Sometimes it's a logistical solution. Sydney one time wrote about wanting dance lessons. They came away from that meeting with dance lessons on the calendar. Once I came to a meeting wanting to go back to Israel so I could take Hebrew lessons. That meeting started the conversation, and we came away with a list of things we would all need to do to pull that off. A few months later I was on my way to Israel!

If you're looking for a way to go one layer deeper into your kid's hearts and desires, we've found this a very effective way to do so.

JOURNAL BELOW:

WRITE WHAT YOU LEARNED, HOW IT WENT, AND WHAT
IMPACT IT'S HAVING ON YOUR FAMILY CULTURE.

3

SIBLING
GIFT GIVING

WAYS TO CONNECT

We've decided to make sibling gift giving a pretty big deal in our house. We have three November birthdays and then right after that is Christmas, so the kids have learned that by September, it's time to save all their money for gifts.

When we were little, this started off as a Christmas thing where Mom and Dad would take us all to a thrift store and take us in one at a time to buy each of our siblings a present. At that stage, Mom and Dad paid for everything, but the point was to get us thinking about each other. Now that Jackson and I can drive we still do it, taking ourselves out to a mall with our own money we've been saving for months, and split into teams to go buy each other presents.

We also get each other birthday presents, and as we've gotten older we've gotten better! It started with Jackson picking out a sword for Kaira and Mom asking, "Now are you sure that's what Kaira wants?"

Some of the most memorable gifts are: Jackson and Sydney buying me the entire hardcover collection of Percy Jackson Heroes of Olympus. I then used that gift to read the whole series to my sisters which they all really enjoyed. Or when Kaira bought Jackson a gift card to "Breakout" an escape room he really wanted to go to, and they got to go together. I got Sydney tickets to a Taylor Swift concert, and Elisa got me a gift card to Color Me Mine, a place where you can paint your own pottery! As you can see, experiences are a great idea because they involve more than one sibling.

Some of the values I've seen with this is: we learn to be generous with our money, we start to notice things siblings like or want and then buy them in advance with an occasion in mind, and Mom and Dad don't have to buy all the gifts! (Gifts are one of my love languages so I can get super into it!)

JOURNAL BELOW:

WRITE WHAT YOU LEARNED, HOW IT WENT, AND WHAT
IMPACT IT'S HAVING ON YOUR FAMILY CULTURE.

4

TV PARTNERS

WAYS TO CONNECT

The Netflix spiral. We all know it well. When it reaches the "Are you still there?" screen, you know you're there.

So we've had different philosophies for T.V. and movies throughout the years. We've never really had cable, and we've had Netflix on and off. The main reason is it's easy for us to have access to a bunch of stuff we shouldn't be watching, and it's easy for all of us to fall into the Netflix death spiral.

T.V. and movies have a ton of benefits, especially when the whole family is together experiencing an epic story. When one child is isolated in their room on their 10th episode of the day, it's not one of those benefits. So we created "T.V. partners."

This requires everyone to have at least one partner when they want to start a new T.V. show. Mom watches a lot of shows with us like Agents of S.H.I.E.L.D., Arrow, Flash, Jericho, etc. Me, Jackson and Sydney watched Once Upon A Time. Sydney, Elisa and Kaira like Miraculous Ladybug. All of us have watched Avatar the Last Airbender repeatedly together... you get the idea.

Since we don't have Netflix, everyone has to buy their own show on iTunes. That way they have a bit of skin in the game. Do they really want to watch that show? How much are you willing to invest?

This also applies on Shabbat which is crucial because otherwise we'd all go off into our little corners on our own devices and get trapped in an endless iTunes movie cycle. This way, if more than one are watching a show or movie, it's usually on a T.V. and makes it easier to keep tabs and tell them when enough is enough. Shabbat is generally the only time we are allowed a three to four episode splurge. If it's on a weekday, it's usually cut off at one or two.

Media is everywhere nowadays, and it's easily recklessly consumed. Keeping a tab on kids and their consumption habits are doing them a favor while not completely cutting them off from ever watching anything.

JOURNAL BELOW:

WRITE WHAT YOU LEARNED, HOW IT WENT, AND WHAT
IMPACT IT'S HAVING ON YOUR FAMILY CULTURE.

5

HIGHS AND LOWS

WAYS TO CONNECT

Even though our family tries to have multiple checkpoints throughout the week, we might not all be aware of how everyone's days are going. So every week at our Sunday morning meeting we will go around and say our high and low for the week. Usually, this also requires us to go over the events of the week so we can reflect on what happened.

On the daily, we have a tendency to only remark on the high parts of the week, or when we do have a bad day, it's hard to talk about, or there isn't a place to talk about it. Usually every week someone's high or low might have been something other members of the family didn't even know was happening.

The highs and lows gives the parents a chance to observe the things that affect or stand out to us kids that they might not be aware of. It also gives us siblings an opportunity to celebrate or empathize with each other.

Another friend of ours does a version of this called 'highs and learns' because he sometimes mentioned the kids would get a little too caught up on the lows and sometimes that'd feel like it set the tone for the exercise. So now they do their favorite moment (highs), and then one thing they learned or were curious about or thought was fascinating in the day.

JOURNAL BELOW:

WRITE WHAT YOU LEARNED, HOW IT WENT, AND WHAT
IMPACT IT'S HAVING ON YOUR FAMILY CULTURE.

6

BIRTHDAY TOASTS

WAYS TO CONNECT

With five kids, birthdays can get a little overwhelming. Especially when three of them are in the same month! We still want them to be unique and meaningful, but we didn't want to plan a blow out birthday party for each of them every year. We used to combine the November birthdays into one party, but then each individual kid didn't feel as celebrated.

So Mom and Dad decided to give each kid (and adult for that matter) a "birthday Shabbat." The way this works is we find the Shabbat closest to their birthday, and we invite the Grandparents as usual, but we also get to invite some friends over. We get to plan the menu, and after dinner, we do presents and dessert, so it's like a mini party built around a rhythm we already have in our schedule.

But what makes it really special are the birthday toasts! We also do this for the grandparent birthdays, our birthdays, our nephew Clayton's birthday, we even do it for anniversaries sometimes.

At a birthday Shabbat, everyone already knows that means they need to think of a toast. Some people even come prepared with something written, but typically it's just in their head. Then throughout the meal someone will clink their glass, say something nice about the birthday person, sometimes it involves tears, then they say what the toast is to. We all say "To _____!" (example: generosity, sense of humor or caring heart, etc.) and then we cheer to the toast!

It's really that simple. But it makes the birthday person feel loved, celebrated, and they have an entire event that revolves around them. We also make the day of their birthday special but the birthday Shabbat is what we have started looking forward to the most.

We didn't start doing this till Jackson and I were a bit older, but that's just cause we hadn't thought about it yet. Kaira (the youngest) was probably around five years old, so I guess you can start it whenever their memories start forming, and they're able to appreciate the things people are saying. Toasts can be short and funny too until they're old enough to break out in tears at the heartfelt speech from Mom (she cries every time).

JOURNAL BELOW:

WRITE WHAT YOU LEARNED, HOW IT WENT, AND WHAT
IMPACT IT'S HAVING ON YOUR FAMILY CULTURE.

7

SHABBAT MONTHLY GETAWAYS

WAYS TO CONNECT

If you find that Shabbatting in your own home isn't restful enough, you'll appreciate this one.

We now live with all my grandparents. Sometimes we have a family living with us too, and everything starts to feel a little crowded. Add to that, we are living in an urban area, and Mom grew up in the country and frequently longs for the flat fields of Ohio.

We decided once a month we'd get away to the country for a Shabbat. Every Shabbat is pretty restful, but this one usually helps recharge even the most depleted of us. You could do this even if you live far from family and decide to go spend a Shabbat closer to them, or if you live in the country and you want a weekend with city vibes and activities. Maybe it's every 6 months, not every month. Really whatever makes the parents feel recharged and ready to tackle the coming weeks is insanely valuable.

What's fun about the trip to the country is that a lot of Airbnb's we have rented don't have wifi and have terrible cell service. One time we actually stayed at a cabin in the middle of a soybean field, and it felt like a lean-to from the 1800s. Some of us kids spent all day playing in the woods, Mom and I literally sat on the ground and watched ants build an anthill for two hours, Dad finished reading a whole book, some of us took naps on a picnic blanket in the grass and all us kids shared one room for two nights. Every night we played group card games, and we packed enough food for the whole weekend. We did take a little excursion to a putt-putt course not far and made an ice cream pit-stop.

The point is, get out, get away, from whatever is normal and do it as often that makes it feel worthwhile to your family and really focus on resting your soul.

JOURNAL BELOW:

WRITE WHAT YOU LEARNED, HOW IT WENT, AND WHAT
IMPACT IT'S HAVING ON YOUR FAMILY CULTURE.

8

CAR
CONVERSATIONS

WAYS TO CONNECT

We all know that awkward moment in the car with your kids. You pick them up from school or take them out to lunch and ask how they are. "Good" they reply. "How was school...do you have homework...what are you thinking about..." can all be dead-end questions that are born of your good intentions but have no true power to draw out that answer you really want to hear. What's really going on inside of your child at that moment?

A useful tool my Dad has used to combat this is a game called the "Ungame." You can get it for different ages, but basically, it's a box of question cards. You can choose different levels of questions depending on how deep you want to go. To incentivize them to answer a question he keeps our favorite gum in his car and so any time they ask for a piece he tells us we need to answer a question first.

We've had really great discussions about dreams (real dreams and also dreams for the future) stirring passions, hard friendships, something annoying that happened that week, if we are having a hard time sleeping, our favorite food, places we want to visit, etc.

The car is often such an unutilized time asset. Most people can multitask while driving and have learned to do so with podcasts and music...but what about with people? This could also be helpful for your spouse if you're having a hard time coming up with just the right question to ask. Maybe you're on your way to your date and don't really know what you're going to talk about. Whip out a card to get the ball rolling!

JOURNAL BELOW:

WRITE WHAT YOU LEARNED, HOW IT WENT, AND WHAT
IMPACT IT'S HAVING ON YOUR FAMILY CULTURE.

9

PLAYLISTS

WAYS TO CONNECT

This one is pretty simple, but it's actually been so helpful for memory-making. Our family doesn't have Spotify because Dad has already bought so many good songs on iTunes and because he likes the music we listen to be considered and thought through, not just thrown together by an automated playlist or "what's hot."

So he carefully buys and curates iTunes songs and playlists based off occasions and activities our family partakes in. We have playlists like:

- Road Trip. Our family used to have an RV, and so this playlist is quite the nostalgic throwback.
- Game Night. Chill, mellow, fun music we all like.
- Sukkot. Mostly worship mixed with a few secular songs I found that play into the theme of this Biblical holiday.
- Shabbat Clean-Up. Our clean up after Shabbat meal is like a big dance party, so this has some fun ones mixed in with some Hebrew songs and crazy worship.
- Tolkien/Fantasy. Perfect for before our book reading on Monday nights.
- Workout. These are the songs I workout to but also the songs the kids can have fun with and dance crazy. Some Just Dance songs are in there cause us girls are wild and memorize the moves to our favorite Just Dance songs just so we can bust it out at parties or spontaneous family dance nights.
- 50's Swing. We occasionally host a swing dance party at our house.
- Various mood playlists like "chill, calm, happy."

I LOVE that we do this because there's a memory we all develop around a specific set of songs. We can hear the first note of "On the Road Again," and all have the exact same memory of driving down our old driveway in the RV off for an adventure. Or "The Song of Durin" and we all think about being huddled around the fire listening to Dad read Tolkien. It's one of the connections siblings have that will last a lifetime, and you can really bring that out in music.

JOURNAL BELOW:

WRITE WHAT YOU LEARNED, HOW IT WENT, AND WHAT
IMPACT IT'S HAVING ON YOUR FAMILY CULTURE.

1

FAMILY
READING TIME

WAYS TO BE A TEAM

We are all familiar with the screen problem. The temptation to sink into individual movies, video games, social media, and YouTube is far harder to battle after dinner when you're full, tired, and have no plans. For that reason, one way we've tried to mitigate against this is to try to schedule some sort of family activity every evening as an alternative. We have a movie night, a Bible Study night, or a youth group we host. One that we probably enjoy the most is Family Reading Night.

This is a pretty simple one and easy to do with all ages. All you really need is 10-30 minutes depending on your attention span, and a book or series everyone enjoys. If you have younger kids, this could just be a short picture book like Dr. Seuss. As they get a little older, maybe you could dive into an easy series like the Magic Tree House then up to Little House on the Prairie, Narnia or even Tolkien!

Dad really loves Tolkien, so that's the one we typically go for. It's a way he can share something he loves with us, and we can enter into a world he often finds himself in. Or it might excite you to dive into something different as a family and discover a new story together.

Challenge: try just one night and see how it goes. Tell the kids earlier in the day, make it short, and make it special with a snack or treat. Then read a special story to your kids tonight for 10 minutes.

The pro tips here are:
- Have activities for them to do as they are listening. Quiet toys, drawing, sewing, fidget objects, etc. This one is huge, and the way we say it in our house is during story time each kid also needs to have a 'hand activity.' We've noticed this keeps much higher morale and joy in the room rather than feeling like pulling teeth. And research has shown you retain and engage with the reading and content much better when your hands are actively involved also!
- Have an end in mind. Let the kids know if this will take 5 minutes, 10 minutes, till the end of the chapter, or if you're going to read the whole book if it's just a picture book.
- Make it interesting! You could read the characters in different voices or have them act it out.

● If there is a movie based on that book, you could get them excited about it by showing them the trailer and then promising you can watch the film as soon as you all read the book. This especially helps with long chapter books if you have younger kids and you want them to want to finish it.

JOURNAL BELOW:

WRITE WHAT YOU LEARNED, HOW IT WENT, AND WHAT IMPACT IT'S HAVING ON YOUR FAMILY CULTURE.

2

MEDIA NIGHT

WAYS TO BE A TEAM

Since we're talking about ways to spend our evenings and screen time...screens aren't all bad. Especially when they are used as a tool in a controlled environment. That's why we implemented media night. One of the things that can happen pretty quickly in the home is when every person seems to be passively watching or being sucked into their own media all the time. One kid is watching YouTube, one kid is watching a movie, and the parent is checking social media. This, of course, is fine and has its place but we like to distinguish between passive consumption in individual settings, vs. engaging in active family activities like a movie night in the home. Not all media time is created equal, and that distinction is always helping in building a family team!

One way we try to do this is once a week we watch something together. Sometimes we are going through a T.V. series as a family, or we watch a really cool movie. It's even a football game sometimes during football season!

This is another way to either share one of your real loves with your kids or find a new one! Two T.V. shows we went through together were: Star Trek: The Next Generation, and Centennial. (Totally recommend Centennial by the way. It's all about a single plot of land in America throughout about 100 years. You get to know characters and family generations all the way from Native Americans to a modern day city.) And yes, we are all major Trekies now!

T.V. shows are great when you know you can all be on media night. It just so happens that my community group started meeting on media night, so I don't always make it. The family either re-watches old Star Trek episodes or movies I don't mind missing.

Movies are a great option when you really want to expose your kids to a specific story. There are some fantastic stories out there that just have to be experienced on the big screen with people you love. A Field of Dreams, Mr. Hollands Opus, The Greatest Showman, Kubo and the Two Strings, The Secret of Kells, Mary Poppins, Anne of Green Gables and The Scarlet Pimpernel are some of our favorites! We usually split one movie into two nights since we only have about an hour allotted for Media Night.

JOURNAL BELOW:

WRITE WHAT YOU LEARNED, HOW IT WENT, AND WHAT
IMPACT IT'S HAVING ON YOUR FAMILY CULTURE.

3

FAMILY
BIBLE STUDY

WAYS TO BE A TEAM

Bible studies makeup about three of our evening activities but in varying ways. The first one is Monday night dinner. We all have the same Bible study schedule we are going through, which will be talked about in a different chapter, but there are five readings a week. We all try to read through all five and then on Monday nights we go out to dinner and discuss what we read. Everyone brings their ESV journaling Bible which makes it easy to flip back to the previous week's passages and look at the notes they took and questions they might have had.

The second Bible study we do is a youth group we host at our house. The other 12-18-year-old kids in our community all come over on Thursday nights. We start with a game, then do a Bible discussion and then snacks. At this point, 4 of the 5 of us fit in that age group and my Dad, along with the other dads, alternate leading the discussion, so most of the family is involved. The conversation usually involves a group reading of the passage, then splitting up in groups to discuss, then coming back as a whole group to ask and answer questions. Or sometimes we mix it up and play "Midrash Roulette" which is just a fancy way of saying, everyone's name gets put in a bowl and after the passage is read Dad pick a name out and they have to say something that stuck out to them. This usually sparks a more significant question or discussion.

The last weekly family Bible study we do is on Friday night after Shabbat. After the meal, once all the dishes are done, everyone retires to the living room where we read a passage and discuss it. Depending on who is involved and attention spans this can last anywhere from 20 minutes to an hour, so do what's best for your family! Also, the way we do it is ideal for older families, but we know a lot of younger families who also do this. It's usually a lot shorter and involves the Jesus Storybook Bible, acting out a skit or asking some brief questions to keep them engaged. But one tip we like to mention across all ages is to pull the Scriptures into your already formed rhythms (for us dinner on Monday and Shabbat on Friday). We are already eating dinner, why not whip out the Scriptures and ask a few questions? Too many times we make this time too formal, and that can easily lead to too much pressure on the parents or lack of joy with the kids. Deuteronomy 6 is also a great chapter to remind to continually remind ourselves that putting the Scriptures at the front of our kids minds and hearts is pivotal to building a family team and can be brought into everyday life!

The main idea with this tool is to have a time and place that your kids are in the Word with you and can dive into some of their questions and deepen their understanding at all ages and stages!

JOURNAL BELOW:

WRITE WHAT YOU LEARNED, HOW IT WENT, AND WHAT IMPACT IT'S HAVING ON YOUR FAMILY CULTURE.

4

GAME NIGHT

WAYS TO BE A TEAM

My Papa is really into board games. Dominos, Monopoly, and Catan are his love languages. One way we have learned to involve him and his hobbies more are giving him Saturday night as game night. Giving a grandparent a fun night or time where they get to be in their element and administer something they love (in this case, board games) is a great way to honor them and also build the multi-generational team.

Usually, Mom and Dad use this as their date night, but us kids all gather up at about 7:00PM and help Papa gather his fun snacks. He always has popcorn, M&Ms, pretzels, and Verners to share which, of course, increases the interest. This also opens a unique opportunity for him to build into us. We laugh together, play together, and have a great connection and conversation throughout. I even remember one night when someone cheated just a tiny bit, and he got to talk to us about honesty and integrity. Other times, something will trigger a childhood memory for him, and he gets to tell us about his past and our family history.

Even if you do this and a grandparent isn't involved, it's an excellent way for you to get to know another part of your kids. See what they're like in a pressure-filled, competitive setting. Now, of course, sometimes unhealthy competition can be detrimental or harmful to team dynamics, but in most cases, board games are the perfect controlled scenario that aren't that high risk, and yet allow things to surface in a perfect way to teach, learn, communicate, and more!

Another reason we do this on a Saturday night is it's a good idea to have something that signifies the end to Shabbat. We've learned if there's no clear end point, what once was a peaceful, soul-restful Sabbath, is now a time to be sluggish and lazy, watch the 6th episode of the day and sink into isolation.

Here are some of our favorites and some ideas of who and what they could be good for!
- Catan (ages 6+, 2-6 players with expansion, strategy, 1 hour+)
- Monopoly (ages 6+, 2-8 players, 1 hour+)
- Mexican Train (ages 5+, 3-8 players, 30 minutes+, uses dominos)
- Hearts (ages 10+, 4 players, 40-80 minutes, strategy, uses cards)
- Euchre (ages 10+, 4 players, 40-80 minutes, strategy, uses cards)
- Ticket to Ride (ages 6+, 2-5 players, 1 hour+)

- Catch Phrase (ages 8+, 6+ players in even numbers, as long as you want)
- Taboo (ages 8+, 6+ players in even numbers, as long as you want)
- Clue (ages 8+, 3-6 players, 1 hour+)
- Rack-o (ages 6+, 4 players, 40 minutes+)
- Dutch blitz (ages 6+, 3-8 players with expansion, 40 minutes+)
- Nertz (ages 6+, 3+ players, 1 hour+)

JOURNAL BELOW:

WRITE WHAT YOU LEARNED, HOW IT WENT, AND WHAT IMPACT IT'S HAVING ON YOUR FAMILY CULTURE.

5

GOSPEL
BIBLE SKITS

WAYS TO BE A TEAM

When your kids are young, it's a challenge to figure out how to help them engage in the Bible.

One way Mom and Dad did this was through having us act out different stories in the Bible. We had a chest of fun costumes and would read an action-packed story from Scripture or a parable, pausing after each statement or action so us kids could act it out.

Afterward, it's great to follow up the skit with a conversation about what we can learn from that story and how it might apply to each of our lives individually.

To take this to the next level, you can search for "Bible skits" on Amazon and find books where lots of stories are broken down into skit form.

It's important to find ways to build spiritual rhythms in every stage of your families life, and a primary key is to develop rhythms where you only have to prep once, and then you can initiate the rhythm on the spot with zero prep afterward. So getting a few costumes and a book should be all you'll need to have a bunch of fun and meaningful times around the Bible with your young kids.

JOURNAL BELOW:

WRITE WHAT YOU LEARNED, HOW IT WENT, AND WHAT
IMPACT IT'S HAVING ON YOUR FAMILY CULTURE.

6

ALL FAMILY SPORTS

WAYS TO BE A TEAM

Sports are a HUGE deal in our culture. And they are great. But we do have to always actively resist or critically think about how certain cultural institutions can help or hurt families. We believe sports can do either. For our family, we realized the allegiance most of us are tempted to give to sports, and the sacrifice we are usually asked to make seems to be much farther than we were comfortable going. And so we said we were not interested in our family going five different directions every night of the week for philosophical but also practical reasons.

But sports are fun, and kids can learn a lot from them, so we didn't want to take that away completely. When we were younger I played basketball, and Jackson played football, but once we realized we couldn't do that for much longer we started looking for sports we could all do together or at least at the same time.

A sports club near us offered group tennis lessons, so that was our first endeavor. Once a week us kids had a class we could all be in with a bunch of other kids. Then once a week we had a private family lesson, and we also went to the park in the summer to play and practice. It was a blast! This was right when Kaira was learning to walk so obviously she couldn't play, but she liked pushing around her little grocery cart to collect the balls and Elisa had more fun bouncing the ball against the wall, but we could all do it together, have fun, and it gave us the experience of playing a sport.

That lasted a year or two, then for a season just the kids took private gymnastics lessons together, but the thing that really stuck was Taekwondo. We found a martial arts school not far from our house that offered great classes but also private lessons. Master Fry was a life saver for us. For two years all seven of us, plus cousin Clayton, went to class twice a week. He even worked around our travel schedule and let us test for the next belt during one of our lessons, so we didn't have to come on Saturday, our day of rest. Mom and Dad stopped right before black belt because it required a lot more commitment and physical requirements, but the rest of us made it to black belt.

All this to say, find something you can all participate in. You can encourage each other when you're having a hard time, celebrate accomplishments together, and you don't have to divide your driving and time between so many members. We realized even coming home and laughing or crying at stories together was a big deal instead of experiencing something alone and not knowing how to convey it to the rest of the family.

We currently don't have an all family sport. Jackson still does Taekwondo and Sydney has since started dance lessons, which they do on the same night. We have turned that into the night where Dad leads a Bible study and Mom teaches classes at her quilt shop. If you have to do something apart from the family, try to make them all happen on the same night so the rest of the week you can be unified!

JOURNAL BELOW:

WRITE WHAT YOU LEARNED, HOW IT WENT, AND WHAT IMPACT IT'S HAVING ON YOUR FAMILY CULTURE.

7

DADDY CHECK-IN

WAYS TO BE A TEAM

Does this sound or feel familiar? You tell your kids to do something over and over again, and they never get around to it? Are you home alone with the kids all day absorbing attitude? You are trying to keep track of each kid's tasks and assignments and whether they were finished correctly or even finished at all? If you relate, you need a Daddy check-in.

This is another thing my Mom struggled with, as I'm sure lots of moms do, and it took some work to figure out how to fix it, but the solution has been perfect. The two younger girls have a notebook where they keep track of their assignments. Each week they make a new chart with the tasks down one side and days across the other side. Mom will remind them in the morning what they need to get done that day and that's the only time she says anything about it.

Then Mom has an alarm on her phone set for every day at 5:30PM to remind her to initiate Daddy check-in. Maybe some dads can initiate it on their own, but my Dad needs a reminder. The girls bring him their notebooks and for each task they finished, he puts a star in its corresponding square. If they didn't finish it, then after dinner he keeps them accountable to stay at the living room table and complete the assignment. After that, he gives them a check mark in the box. If they get a certain amount of stars a week, it equals a small prize.

We found it valuable not to make that prize equal time with Mom or Dad. We don't want them to think they need to accomplish something to earn an outing with a parent or that they needed to work for their attention. Dad also stays away from competition. Nothing breaks down team spirit like competition within the team. You don't want your kids to have any reason not to want their sibling to succeed.

This kind of tool lets dads be the backstop. Especially in a family where mom is home more with the kids, the dad needs a time where he shoulders that job and really challenges his kids to rise to what he knows they are capable of doing.

Also, their list of tasks was pretty long since it included the entirety of their home-schooling, but if your kids attend a school, their tasks could be their homework. Really it's anything you as a parent feel like they should be able to complete without a reminder and be held accountable to it at the end of the day.

So this helped Dad stay connected to what his kids were doing through the day, and let Mom feel like she didn't need to nag constantly. She could offer a friendly reminder and be hands off. This works best for kids 7 and older because when they're younger, you obviously want to be pretty hands on. But if you're trying to teach them self-motivation, not to procrastinate, or accountability, we have found this method helpful.

(If I'm being honest, I wish we came up with this idea when I was in school! My Enneagram 1 personality would have loved to have a checklist to show off to my Dad every single day!)

JOURNAL BELOW:

WRITE WHAT YOU LEARNED, HOW IT WENT, AND WHAT IMPACT IT'S HAVING ON YOUR FAMILY CULTURE.

....

....

....

....

....

....

....

8

TAKING KIDS TO WORK

WAYS TO BE A TEAM

This is going to sound highly impractical for a lot of you, and maybe it is, but we wanted to encourage you right off the bat to consider alternative avenues of integration when it comes to involving your kids in your work life. It's where you spend your time, your energy and it's where you provide from them. You also probably have a lot of relationships there. It's strange to think of how little most kids know about what their Dad does all day long. It didn't always use to be this way, but we've gotten so used to it we sort of don't question it. And not all our jobs are conducive to bringing our kids to work in large capacities, but I do think every person can ask how can I just take one more small step forward towards integration with my work and kids?

So here are some ways this has looked for us throughout the years.

The way my parents started involving us kids in their work was out of necessity. They were starting an online e-commerce business in our basement and needed labels put on merchandise. We loved it, and there was a reward system set up for how many labels we could put on. (I know... we use reward systems?? You'd never guess.)

Next Dad had a "work from home job" but didn't really like working from home. He needed to change up the environment and move around a bit. So each kid had a day they went with him, or sometimes we'd go together. We'd go to libraries, coffee shops, and restaurants all day, which was awesome. We even told people, "Yeah my Dad works at Starbucks." Not realizing that most people wouldn't understand what we were trying to say! I have some of my favorite nostalgic memories from this period. I first learned how to use chopsticks when Dad and I would go to our favorite Japanese restaurant on my day with him. I also got special drinks to myself, I could spend all day reading my favorite Fairy books, I got to know what my Dad did for work, be a part of his meetings, and have long car conversations.

Now he has to stay pretty close to his office. He comes and goes for some meetings, but for the most part, he stays put, so it isn't quite as exciting, but we still go with him because we even find it easier to focus. It keeps us motivated to have a certain number of things done before we get home.

His office also has a fun morning once a week where the whole leadership cooks breakfast for everyone, so he usually brings some of the girls to help cook. His company also brings in interns every summer so our family will always host them for dinner one evening. He has each intern talk about what they do at work, where they're from, and where they see themselves going. It helps us get to know them and to educate and inspire us kids.

So whatever your work or their school situation is, the main point of this chapter is to involve your kids in your work or educate them about what you do as much as possible. Make them feel like the family is a part of your work mission, not just you!

JOURNAL BELOW:

WRITE WHAT YOU LEARNED, HOW IT WENT, AND WHAT IMPACT IT'S HAVING ON YOUR FAMILY CULTURE.

9

LEARNING A FOREIGN LANGUAGE AS A FAMILY

WAYS TO BE A TEAM

Our family has had a specific calling to Israel, dating back to when Mom and Dad first met in Jerusalem. Because of this, they wanted us to learn Hebrew. Lots of schools have required foreign language credits, usually Spanish, French, or German. Since we were homeschooled, Mom and Dad could choose what language we learned, and they decided on one we would actually have a lot of opportunities to learn and use-Hebrew. Our whole family has lived in Israel for months at a time, it came in handy, and all seven of us have learned a lot. Whatever language you decide, it is an excellent way for people and your family to connect.

When learning a foreign language in America, it can be hard to find other people who speak that language. If you are all learning the same language, you can help each other, practice with each other, and study at the same time. The whole mission part is an added bonus. Do you go on mission trips as a family? Does one of your kids have a heart for another country? Do you have adopted kids? Do you know an immigrant family? Do you sponsor an international child? These are all great ways to decide what language to pursue.

That being said there are multiple ways you can learn a language:
- Find a native and ask for private lessons
- Public/private schools
- Homeschool co-ops
- Rosetta Stone
- eTeacher or another online tutor
- Duolingo
- If you spend significant time in that country, learn while you're there and USE IT no matter how embarrassing it feels

These are all things we have tried and that work great! It just depends on what phase of language learning you are in and what works for you family in that season!

JOURNAL BELOW:

WRITE WHAT YOU LEARNED, HOW IT WENT, AND WHAT
IMPACT IT'S HAVING ON YOUR FAMILY CULTURE.

10

SCRIPTURE
SCHEDULE

WAYS TO BE A TEAM

How do you keep your kids motivated to read their Bible? What should you encourage them to read? How can you initiate conversations about what they're learning in the Word? These questions are the reason we came up with our Scripture schedule.

All Dad did was split the Bible into its 5 parts: Torah, Writings, Prophets, Gospel, Epistles. Some sections are on 2-year cycles, some 3 years. Each week there is a reading in each section.

EXAMPLE

Week ends	Torah (2 yr)	Prophets (3 yr)	Writings (3 yr)	Gospels (2 yr)	Epistles (2 yr)
Sat, Oct 29, 2016	Genesis 1-2	Jeremiah 50-52	Daniel 7-8	Luke 14	Romans 1
Sat, Nov 5, 2016	Genesis 3	Ezekiel 1-3	Daniel 9-10	Luke 15-16	Romans 2
Sat, Nov 12, 2016	Genesis 4-5	Ezekiel 4-7	Daniel 11-12	Luke 17	Romans 3
Sat, Nov 19, 2016	Genesis 6-7	Ezekiel 8-10	Ezra 1-2	Luke 18	Romans 4

Every time Dad prints out the schedule on one piece of paper for each person it can fit about 5-6 months worth of readings. The first time we did it, Mom and Dad promised us a massive prize if we could finish the entire page. Coincidently, the page ended in December, so it ended up being a family Christmas trip to Florida. If we hadn't finished it, we had to pay for our own ticket (two of the kids ended up having to pay for their own ticket).

It's important to us that Bible reading doesn't become religious or legalistic, we want to want to read it. But it's also useful to add an incentive at first as a motivator, and it helps it become a habit. We don't have a huge prize for completing a page anymore, but every Monday dinner is our "Midrash

Monday Meal" where we go out to dinner, and everyone brings their Bible. Then we talk about what we read that week. When everyone is reading the same thing, it helps to initiate conversations because you're familiar with the same passage. This keeps us accountable weekly to not only read but pay attention to our reading and take notes if we have any questions.

If I'm being honest, this is still something we're trying to really figure out. Kaira and I are pretty good at sticking to our schedule, (or at least catching up when we do get behind) but the middle three kids, who are all in school and have a ton of homework, quickly push it to the side. When Mom and Dad see this happening they opt for the heart-to-heart convo instead of a reward/consequence system approach. Again, we want everyone to want to read the Bible or see it as a priority, not homework.

JOURNAL BELOW:

WRITE WHAT YOU LEARNED, HOW IT WENT, AND WHAT IMPACT IT'S HAVING ON YOUR FAMILY CULTURE.

11
GRANDPARENT STORIES

WAYS TO BE A TEAM

Back before our grandparents came over every week for Shabbat, when we were trying to incorporate them slowly in small ways, we would invite them to Shabbat about once a month and ask them to prepare a story to share with the kids. They were all really good at it but Mom's Dad, Grandpa-Don, got super into it. He would prepare for weeks, gathering old pictures, writing small biographies on ancestors or stories from his childhood. He would often come with packets all ready for the grandkids to take away.

These have become especially important to all of us after he passed away, and since then I think we have all realized how cherished these moments and memories really are.

Now, it's slightly less formal, but since they all come to every Shabbat, it gives us the chance to remember with them events that happened on specific dates. For instance, on Veterans Day, Papa will tell us stories about being in the Army, on Grammy's parent's birthdays she likes to make a slideshow to show us and tell stories about them. And Julie, Mom's Mom, works with the girls in their Quilt Shop, so she's always telling stories about her mother and sisters and what things were like back in her day. On anniversaries they talk about how they met, their wedding, or something from their newlywed years.

When your kids ask the question, "Where did I come from?" "Who am I?" "Why is so-and-so like this?" They shouldn't have to look too far for an answer. It's okay to tell them "You are Sydney Grace Pryor, daughter of April, granddaughter of Julie, great-granddaughter of Eloise and William, who was a dairy farmer." or "You come from generations of believers on one side of your family and on the other side of your family, this is who was the first Christian, and this is why and how it happened." They take it on as part of their identity and have something to build their story off of. They don't need to start from ground zero. They're standing on the shoulders of countless generations. Show them who those generations are.

JOURNAL BELOW:

WRITE WHAT YOU LEARNED, HOW IT WENT, AND WHAT
IMPACT IT'S HAVING ON YOUR FAMILY CULTURE.

12

RITES OF PASSAGE

WAYS TO BE A TEAM

Our culture has a hard time not understanding that children need to know where they came from. We believe kids need to find themselves, independent of any identity shaping by the family, so we fail to create the kinds of events that help kids understand who they are in the family story. One of the results of this is a lack of "rites of passage." It's important to commemorate different events in a child's life to show them they have a family and a team around them, not only supporting them but also giving them a legacy. Here are a few rites of passage our family has developed over the years:

Age 5-Mom and Dad honestly came up with this one because they were tired of continually being asked for gum and pop. They're filled with sugar and not that good for you, so they didn't want to have to evaluate if it was worth it every time the urge came for one of us to ask. So they came up with the rule that you can't chew gum or drink pop until you are 5 years old. And then you can only have gum on Saturdays and pop on Sundays. They didn't mean for this to become a rite of passage, but it sort of did. During our birthday tradition of breakfast in bed, at age 5 we started putting a piece of gum on the tray, and we really got excited about achieving such a rite.

Age 10-Dad's Dad, Jerry or "Papa," decided when each of the grandkids turned 10 years old, he wanted to take them out on a special date. He gave his life to Christ when he was 10 years old, so he sees it as a pivotal age. He took each of his grandkids to do something fun and tell them the story of how he got saved and talk about our faith. All of us Pryor kids have gotten to experience this now, and we all come away with great memories of our Papa.

Age 13- This is the big "coming of age" ceremony where the entire family comes around. We do this on Mom's side of the family, and since there are nearly 30 grandkids, we combine the parties when multiple kids are turning 13 in one year. All of Mom's siblings and their kids come together in a party initiated by her Mom and Dad. Grandpa-Don, Mom's Dad, place his hands on the birthday kids and says, "You don't have to wonder where you came from. You know who you are." And then her Mom, Julie, gives them a generational gift from one of their ancestors. It's become quite a big deal, and a bit harder to do since Grandpa has passed away, but it's a legacy he has left that we still pass on to each grandchild.

Then there are obviously the more normal ones that aren't as generationally impacted, like driving when you're 16, etc. But having something for each kid to have a memory around a specific moment in time when they were given a privilege or something was passed down was very important to us.

JOURNAL BELOW:

WRITE WHAT YOU LEARNED, HOW IT WENT, AND WHAT IMPACT IT'S HAVING ON YOUR FAMILY CULTURE.

13

RESTAURANT GAMES

WAYS TO BE A TEAM

No one likes waiting for their food at a restaurant. On top of that, no one likes waiting for their food at a restaurant with kids. If you have little kids, you may have trouble keeping them occupied, and if they're big kids, they may slip into phone-zone.

Dad did a bit of research and found a few fun group games on his phone for us to do as a family at restaurants. Most of them involve passing the phone around and everyone getting a turn. There is no need to be super loud or disruptive, and it's entertaining and educational.

- Trivia Party! Team quiz game (our fav)
- Guess Word! Party up charades
- Outbursts-guess the word or phrase
- Phrase Party!
- Quiz now-fun tests and quizzes
- Heads Up

And just to incentivize you, consider this. We once had our expensive dinner covered by a stranger who saw our family having fun and talking together. You never know who you will have an impact on!

JOURNAL BELOW:

WRITE WHAT YOU LEARNED, HOW IT WENT, AND WHAT IMPACT IT'S HAVING ON YOUR FAMILY CULTURE.

14

SNACKY DINNER

WAYS TO BE A TEAM

You know those nights when you forgot to plan dinner, or you don't feel like making anything?

These are our favorite nights because we'll go to Mom and Dad around 7PM, starving, asking why we haven't eaten yet. Mom and Dad throw up their hands in surrender and say, "I don't care, just go eat something." And we all run to the kitchen yelling "snacky dinner!!!!"

Before they can regulate anything, Nutella sandwiches are being made, three types of pasta, milkshakes of various flavors, cereal, platters of cheese and crackers, OJ, pop and a handful of other things they would typically never be okay with at dinner time.

Now, Dad is usually very particular about our dinners. Most are eaten together, and we have a meat, a cooked vegetable, a starch, and a salad. We meal plan and grocery shop for specific ingredients for healthy meals thought through a week in advance.

But there come those evenings when you "just can't even." As parents, you don't want to cook. You don't care what your kids ingest. You kind of just want to be alone with your spouse and missing one meal around the table that month isn't going to be awful.

So yeah, snacky dinners are definitely the lazy route, but it gives us a break, uses up some food in the pantry, and us kids get excited about it.

JOURNAL BELOW:

WRITE WHAT YOU LEARNED, HOW IT WENT, AND WHAT
IMPACT IT'S HAVING ON YOUR FAMILY CULTURE.

1

ONE IMPROVEMENT PER WEEK

WAYS TO IMPROVE

If you feel like there's a lot of tiny things that pile up throughout the week, and you're the only one that notices them, or if you don't feel like there's a rhythmic check-in time with your spouse where you can bring these problems up...we have come up with a solution to this problem.

It fits best during our weekly Sunday morning family meeting. Dad'll ask Mom what one thing was about the week that didn't go well. It has been many things: the kitchen is always a mess, the kids are always nagging each other, I don't like how isolated the kids are throughout the day, people leave their stuff out everywhere, I have four teenagers, and yet I'm still cleaning up after all of them! It's usually a pattern she has noticed a problem in, not necessarily a one-time-experience.

So then, as a family, we try to think of creative solutions to those problems. In fact, many of the "creative ways" in this book came out of these discussions. Things like: Kitchen Blitz, Allowance Check-In, Daddy Check-In, Cleaning Zones and many more.

The key to making these systems work is to have a reward and correction. If you read the "Marble System" chapter, you're familiar with these terms. You might be used to rewarding your kids with huge gifts or big outings, and disciplining them for severe disobedience. There also needs to be an in- between. We call these rewards and corrections, and they are great for training drills like these.

I'll use the Kitchen Blitz for example (read that chapter for a more in-depth explanation). Everyone is responsible for cleaning the kitchen once that week, and there is a whiteboard with a checkbox next to your name to keep track. If we make it to the next Sunday meeting and you don't have a checkmark, you owe $5 to the fun jar (once we have enough money we'll go do something fun with the fun jar money). If you do have a check, you get a treat of some kind. You'll be surprised how well sweets works even with teenagers!

Now after a week or two in the training process of this new system, we'll usually take the reward away just because it should become a habit and the reason for cleaning the kitchen should be to serve the family, not to get candy.

Last week something that came up was the younger girls not waking up when they're supposed to. So we had to keep an accountability chart for them. This is a document Mom made and then printed and it's hanging in our kitchen. The top has a description of what it means to be ready for the day and the things they need to have done (brush hair, eat breakfast, Bible time, etc.) so there's no miscommunication. Then under it is a chart for each week of the month. Each month has the names of the three younger girls on one side and the days of the week across the top. Each day of the week has what time they are supposed to be ready by. Every day when they are ready, they write what time they finished by in the corresponding block. At the bottom of the page is a consequence for each person if the chart is either not filled out or if they filled it out but were late.

EXAMPLE

Getting ready for the day means: Get dressed, brush hair and teeth, eat breakfast, read Bible.

Week 1

TIME	Sunday 9:00	Monday 7:00	Tuesday 8:00	Wed. 7:00	Thursday 8:00	Friday 8:00
Sydney	8:56	7:05	8:00	6:55		8:00
Elisa	8:30	7:00	8:10		7:59	7:55
Kaira	8:55	6:58	8:00	7:00	7:54	7:59

Sydney-Filled out but not on time = Loose phone for 12 hours.
Not filled out = Loose phone 24 hours.

Elisa-Filled out but not on time = Loose mp3 for 12 hours.
Not filled out = Loose mp3 24 hours.

Kaira- Filled out but not on time = No computer for 12 hours.
Not filled out = No computer 24 hours.

So a review for one weekly improvement: Ask "what went wrong this week", identify the pattern, work together to create a system to ensure that pattern doesn't continue, create a reward and a correction for the system, after a few weeks take away the reward but maintain an accountability or correction to ensure the desired outcome still happens.

JOURNAL BELOW:

WRITE WHAT YOU LEARNED, HOW IT WENT, AND WHAT IMPACT IT'S HAVING ON YOUR FAMILY CULTURE.

2

BLANKET TIME

WAYS TO IMPROVE

This obviously is one that isn't probably super pertinent if you are out of the toddler stage, but the principle (structured, silent, alone time) is forever necessary, and maybe you can pass this tip-off to a friend who still has little ones.

We will say this one was crucial for Mom, after kid three, to not lose her sanity. She wanted to have time with the Lord in the morning but wasn't always able to wake up before the kids. How could she have a quiet moment alone with three kids running around continually needing her?

Blanket time came out of that need. Each of the kids had our own blanket we had made (basically just two pieces of fleece knotted together at the edges) and they were all different animal prints, so that made it fun. She would have us all go get our blankets, lay it on the floor, and get a bag of toys and books that was ONLY for blanket time. That part is crucial because it helped us look forward to blanket time. All toys had to be silent, and we weren't allowed to leave our blanket.

This tool is so helpful on so many different levels, but it's definitely in the 'training' toolbox. It takes work to implement this one, but the fruit is worth it!

At the very beginning, it involved a lot of training, so it wasn't necessarily "quiet time." She would set the timer for 5 minutes, have us sit on our blanket quietly playing. She would maybe even let us see the timer, so we didn't keep asking how much time was left. Every day she would add an extra minute or two until she was getting in a full 20-30 minutes of Bible reading, journaling, or prayer without interruption. Sometimes this was followed by a fun snack as a reward. Give them something to look forward to if they successfully are still and quiet for 20 minutes! If you have a kid that just won't sit, using your preferred method of effective discipline might be necessary.

This tool became helpful for another time of day as well. Some people call it the witching hour. Or just the plain old difficult hour right before dinner. Where a lot of collisions seem to be happening. It's around 4 or 5PM, you're trying to cook, the kids have energy after naps, but you don't. There's laundry to fold, the house is a disaster, and your husband isn't home yet, you're just trying to STAY SANE. It's a good time to whip out the blanket time. Seriously, just put the blankets on the kitchen floor and have them play quietly, maybe play some fun music or give them a snack to eat on the blanket. Trust me, this 20 minutes to bust out dinner or pick up the house might just save your life.

And guys, this has so many long term benefits as well. It trains your kids to sit still and keep themselves entertained. They get better at sitting through church services or going to a friend's house for dinner. You can involve them in community worship times or other events that you weren't able to before. It's worth the week or two it takes to train them.

JOURNAL BELOW:

WRITE WHAT YOU LEARNED, HOW IT WENT, AND WHAT IMPACT IT'S HAVING ON YOUR FAMILY CULTURE.

3

MARBLE SYSTEM

WAYS TO IMPROVE

This was a crucial part of our family culture for about 10 years and had numerous benefits.

Mom and Dad were well acquainted with various disciplines when we acted up, and they loved giving us huge rewards and displaying their love for us in different, significant ways. But there was this in between that was missing. They wondered how they could give us little rewards for things like obeying right away, helping our sibling put their shoes on, or showing initiative. They tried to figure out how they could gently correct when we rolled our eyes, excluded our siblings or didn't listen right away.

The marble system was super helpful for those times. Basically, what they did was get some marbles or glass beads (you can use anything really). The main requirement is that the kids can physically touch them. The marbles were poured into a big bowl, and then each of us had a bowl or a jar. Every time we did something they wanted to reward, we got to put a marble in our bowl. Every time we did something requiring a correction we had to take a marble out. You could use something not tactile, like tally marks, but there's something about the act of putting a marble in or out of a bowl that was much more satisfying. We also thought about sticker charts, but those are harder to take off.

Some rules:
- You cannot ask for a marble.
- You cannot point out an act of initiative, the parent has to notice it.
- You can't tell a sibling to put a marble in or take a marble out of their bowl or suggest to a parent that a sibling should lose a marble.

A value was attached to the marbles. 10 marbles = ice cream, 20 marbles = book, 30 marbles = toy.

A benefit from this system was that Mom and Dad didn't really foresee was teaching delayed gratification. Every time we got to 10, we would want to get the ice cream, and we'd never get higher so when our bowl was empty, Mom would make us commit to a goal. If we were trying to get a toy, when they got to 10 and were tempted to spend our marbles, she would remind us of what we were saving up for and not let us spend it till we reached our goal. Once we finally bought that toy, we realized the benefits of waiting to get something more significant.

JOURNAL BELOW:

WRITE WHAT YOU LEARNED, HOW IT WENT, AND WHAT
IMPACT IT'S HAVING ON YOUR FAMILY CULTURE.

4

MORNING AND BEDTIME CHECKLISTS

WAYS TO IMPROVE

Picture this: Bedtime is rolling around, it's 8:00 at night, dad got home from work and pulled himself together enough to interact at the dinner table, mom has spent all day with the kids and is tired of dealing with attitudes. A part of you dreads getting the kids ready for bed. It's chaotic, and more like wrangling cats than getting kids to listen.

Maybe you don't have this problem, but perhaps you're like my Dad, and you just want your kids to get themselves ready magically. This one requires some training up front but once they get used to it...it is magical.

And it's pretty simple: make a checklist they can see and cross off themselves. There is something about an external picture that takes away the micro battles between parent and child.

Mom is a checklist queen, so this came pretty naturally to her. She had each of us create our own chart. One side of the paper is for the morning, and the other side is for the night. Along the top are the days of the week and along the side are the tasks. The kids that could read wrote theirs, and the kids that couldn't, drew pictures.

For bedtime it was things like: go potty, brush your teeth, floss, jammies on, clothes in the dirty clothes basket, pick out an outfit for tomorrow.

For morning it was things like: go potty, brush your teeth, brush your hair, jammies in the dirty clothes basket, get dressed.

Mom even got the charts laminated, and we each had a dry erase marker so each week we could erase and start over.

Having us kids get ourselves ready for bed saved Mom and Dad a lot of time and energy so that once we were ready, they could go up and tuck us in. Bedtime turned a 20-minute routine into a 5-minute one.

This starts to be helpful when your oldest is around 5 years old and can help the younger ones, but a lot of that is up to your discretion. If we weren't ready by the alloted time limit, there was a discipline (usually "take a marble out of your bowl"). Obviously, there were the nights that an argument would break out, or someone would have a meltdown and Dad would need to get involved, but the nights' none of that happened were beneficial enough to stick to it.

Mom also loved this for the mornings because we would come downstairs for breakfast already ready for the day! Starting and ending your days right is so important because, well, you do it every day.

JOURNAL BELOW:

WRITE WHAT YOU LEARNED, HOW IT WENT, AND WHAT IMPACT IT'S HAVING ON YOUR FAMILY CULTURE.

....

....

....

....

....

....

....

....

....

5

BED BASKETS
(KEEPING KIDS
IN BED)

WAYS TO IMPROVE

When your kid graduates from cribs to toddler beds it becomes harder to keep them in their room. Especially if your nap times were holy hours like they were for my parents.

Mom and Dad kept us in our room for two hours an afternoon even if we didn't fall asleep. So needless to say, they needed a way for us to occupy ourselves if we weren't tired.

Bed baskets were small baskets each of us had, with toys or books (mostly books) we were only allowed to use during nap time or before bed. That's it, really pretty simple.

For nap times, Mom just wanted us in our rooms, not necessarily in bed, so we had a bit more flexibility there. But for bedtimes, they told us we had to stay in bed starting at around 8PM, and if we weren't tired, we could play with our bed basket stuff. But we HAD to stay in bed. That was important since most of us shared rooms, so they didn't want us disturbing our siblings. The bed basket usually included a book-light or flashlight if it was dark.

So if you're trying to keep your kids in bed, either for naptime or bedtime, fill a basket with books and toys that are reserved for that time only. Sometimes we would even go to the library, pick out books we were super excited about and put those in our bed basket. That changed up the contents of the basket enough and made it really exciting.

JOURNAL BELOW:

WRITE WHAT YOU LEARNED, HOW IT WENT, AND WHAT IMPACT IT'S HAVING ON YOUR FAMILY CULTURE.

6

COMMUNITY
BABYSITTER

WAYS TO IMPROVE

So this one is something Mom did for a few years that gave her a lot of life and was super productive.

We had a solid community of families with kids similar ages to our kids. Mom and the other moms of our community were realizing that it was hard to do things like plan doctors appointments, write the grocery list, manage calendars, return phone calls, etc. while at home.

What they ended up doing was taking all the kids to one person's house (usually our house) and hiring about 2-3 babysitters for like 8-10 kids. They would all go to Starbucks for 2-3 hours with their cookbooks, address books, grocery lists, and calendars and just pump it out (yes, this was before everyone had their own laptop). This really helped her feel connected in terms of "we're in this thing together" with the other ladies in our community. They had a chance to socialize a little bit, exchange ideas, recipes, and such.

The best part was doing it with friends. They actually had a fun time, and we were with all of our friends, so it was like a big play date! Granted, I was always the oldest kid, but I was never one to pass up an opportunity to exercise "the authority of the oldest" and play "babysitters favorite" by keeping everyone else in line.

Stress levels went way down when Mom knew she had that planning time to look forward to.

I asked Mom to say a few words about this:
"A lot of us were pregnant at the same time during this season. We took pictures together with our pregnant bellies, all lined up. Now those kids are teenagers! Crazy to think about. When you find other people who are willing to live life this way, try to push into hard things, go against what mainstream culture has to say, they are worth keeping as friends! We have many relationships that have been around for 10+ years, and it is delightful and encouraging to watch them live out what it means to be a multi-generational team on mission."

JOURNAL BELOW:

WRITE WHAT YOU LEARNED, HOW IT WENT, AND WHAT
IMPACT IT'S HAVING ON YOUR FAMILY CULTURE.

7

TRAFFIC SAFETY

WAYS TO IMPROVE

This one you might think, "Duh," but this is just one of those things that takes no time or energy to implement but could make things way less stressful (those are the best ones, right?).

This can be as simple as a family trip to the grocery store, but we actually encountered it a lot when we traveled too. We'd be at Disney or walking down a foreign street, Mom and Dad trying to keep hands on everyone at once, head on a swivel, trying to keep they four eyes on five people at once all while trying to figure out where we were going.

Seriously...so stressful.

Their solution was so simple you might laugh but it made it so much easier. One of them was assigned as the leader and one was assigned as the caboose. Us kids had to be holding hands with each other or a parent and had to be between the two parents. That way one of them could be focused on where we were going and one was focused on making sure all the ducks were in a row.

This was especially helpful when we were in Israel because lots of the sidewalks were so narrow we had to walk in single file lines anyway. Having Dad to part the Red Sea of people and the kids all holding each other's hands and Mom making sure no one got run over made it much easier to navigate and helped it be easier for us to all go out and do things as a family.

JOURNAL BELOW:

WRITE WHAT YOU LEARNED, HOW IT WENT, AND WHAT
IMPACT IT'S HAVING ON YOUR FAMILY CULTURE.

8

ALLOWANCE CHECK-IN

WAYS TO IMPROVE

Mom and Dad chose to give us a weekly allowance based on our age. If we are 15, we get $15...etc. It also wasn't tied to any task or chore. The reason for that was because we were expected to contribute to the household in many ways, including chores. We were taught to do all of those things regardless if we were getting paid or not. They also wanted a way to bless us, give us something to steward, and to learn about money early. They really wanted us to learn to be good kingdom citizens with our stewardship. So that's why we started making allowances.

They quickly discovered that handing out money every week was a messy affair. Some kids would claim they hadn't received their allowance from the week prior, and some would go into debt promising to pay each other back at an undisclosed time and place. We were also spending our money on menial things.

Mom is the one who remembered her thoughtful and disciplined training as a kid where her Dad bought them each a ledger and taught them to keep track of every single penny that went in and out of their pocket.

So we created an Allowance Check-In, which happens every Sunday after our morning meeting. All of us have a ledger and learned how to write down every time we are given an allowance, spend money, or owe someone something. Dad also had Mom get a carbon copy receipt book from Staples so she could provide us with a receipt with each allowance. This got rid of all the, "I need my allowance from last week too because you forgot" conversations. "Do you have a receipt?" Then you got your allowance last week.

Also, we don't get our allowance unless we can show Mom that the money matches our ledger to the penny. It has trained us to keep our receipts after purchases, look carefully at what we are spending money on, stay accountable to the debts we owe, and plan ahead.

It's a reasonably simple system now, but it took a bit of figuring out at the beginning. Hopefully, this is a help to the parents of teens out there!

JOURNAL BELOW:

WRITE WHAT YOU LEARNED, HOW IT WENT, AND WHAT
IMPACT IT'S HAVING ON YOUR FAMILY CULTURE.

9

PET OWNERS

WAYS TO IMPROVE

Whether we should or should not get a pet was an ongoing conversation in our house since Mom and Dad got married. Dad always had a dog growing up, so he was all for it. And since Jackson is the only boy, he always wanted one. But Mom, understandably, didn't want to get stuck being the one taking care of it in addition to her five kids. We also traveled a lot, so the logistics got complicated quickly.

After our days of traveling for months on end were over, we finally decided to get Jackson a dog for his birthday; it was a HUGE deal. Dad found a breeder and got him a mini aussiedoodle that he named Magnus. The circumstances leading up to us also buying a cat for Sydney the next day is a long story...but yeah, that happened. Then we got Elisa some chickens. So after 17 years of no pets, we suddenly had six.

What made Dad give in was the realization that pets are a great way to train your kids how to become parents themselves someday. Every time the kids lost patience, neglected their pet or took shortcuts, Mom and Dad could see weak spots in their character that they could work on. If it is important to you that your children become great parents, pets are a great tool.

But a word of warning—you have to be prepared to coach your kids through the challenges of pet ownership because as soon as you step in and take over, the pet will begin to shift to become your responsibility. And unless that's what you want, you'll have to be ready to hold the line.

For this reason, Mom and Dad chose to wait until we were entering our teenage years to begin this. And one other major tip. If you want to use pet ownership for this reason, it has to be 100% the pet of just one of your kids. You might have heard the phrase "If two people are responsible, no one is responsible." Having a family pet is excellent but if you want to use a pet to teach your kids responsibility, make it their pet alone and coach them as they learn to shoulder caring for another living being.

JOURNAL BELOW:

WRITE WHAT YOU LEARNED, HOW IT WENT, AND WHAT
IMPACT IT'S HAVING ON YOUR FAMILY CULTURE.

10

CHORE PACKS

WAYS TO IMPROVE

This was a helpful chore system for a really long time. For those of you who don't know, my Mom is super organized. She's very thorough and thoughtful and came up with our chore pack system.

Now really, I think she stole this idea from someone online, but she adapted it to work for our family. What's nice about it is it's easy to dress up or dress down. I'll explain that in a second.

So basically all of the kids got little clip-on name tags, the kind you can slip pieces of paper into. Then Mom got one of those accordion index card holders and wrote chores on cards. This sounds easy, but she actually went the complicated route. This is what I meant about dressing up or dressing down. If you're easily intimidated by lists, charts, and routines then make this as simple as possible. All you need to do is come up with a list of things in the house you want to be cleaned, break it up by child, and then by day of the week. The index card holder is labeled by day of the week so on Monday, Sydney can reach in, find her 2-3 chore cards paper clipped together, slip it into her nametag, clip the nametag to her shirt and go do the chores.

That's the easy version...Mom actually had a massive spreadsheet of things that needed to be cleaned annually, quarterly, monthly, bi-weekly, weekly and daily. Then she figured out which month, week, or day everything should happen that made sense with our schedule.

So those are the two routes for chore packs. You can make it as complicated as Mom did if you feel like that's what you need, or you're good at. Or you can just come up with a few quick chore cards that your kids do as often as you want them to!

JOURNAL BELOW:

WRITE WHAT YOU LEARNED, HOW IT WENT, AND WHAT
IMPACT IT'S HAVING ON YOUR FAMILY CULTURE.

11

CLEANING ZONES

WAYS TO IMPROVE

There is nothing worse than the tragedy of the commons. The occurrence of a shared space that is continuously in chaos because everyone assumes the mess is someone else's responsibility.

So we invented zones. Basically, each of us kids has a few common areas of the house that we are in charge of keeping clean. 2-3 times a week we have what we call "work block" where everyone tackles their zones. For example, I have the kitchen and basement, Jackson has the living rooms, entryway, and office, Elisa has the bathrooms...etc.

The key to this one is each child has to clean up their zone, even if it isn't their mess. They won't like it at first, and it will feel like a grievous injustice, but here is the "why": you need them to realize that every day they accidentally leave evidence of their existence around other common areas. And there is another sibling or parent cleaning up after them. Rather than have each sibling go through the house and try and collect all of their belongings and possibly miss something, they are given a specific zone to make spotless, regardless of whose fault the mess was. And they can live with cleaning up after someone else because in another area of the house someone else is cleaning up after them.

We've found this to be extremely helpful in creating a clear and set area of ownership for each child. We are responsible for its state and having set times for "work block" that we have all built into our rhythm gets rid of the "I didn't have enough time to clean it" argument.

JOURNAL BELOW:

WRITE WHAT YOU LEARNED, HOW IT WENT, AND WHAT
IMPACT IT'S HAVING ON YOUR FAMILY CULTURE.

12

POST-IT
NOTE PICK-UP

WAYS TO IMPROVE

Okay, so this was one of our many inventions to fix the problem of the "tragedy of the commons." While our zones were our ultimate solution, Post-It Note Pick-Up was excellent training for us kids in taking responsibility for our own belongings.

We were having the problem, as so many families do, that once a child was finished with something (toy, project, dish, etc.) they would stand up and walk away, leaving their mess behind. Mom and Dad were pretty fed up with it so here was our solution:

Mom would walk around with a stack of mini post-it notes in her pocket throughout the day. If she ever saw an object that clearly belonged to somebody, she would tag it with a post-it note labeled with their initials. Then she'd go over to the whiteboard with everyone's names and put a tally under that person's name. The post-it was to signify that they got tallied for that object and they needed to clean it up.

At the end of the week, if the whole family added five or fewer tallies, we got to go see a movie. If the entire family had 10 or less, we got a Hershey Kiss, and any more than 10 would have no reward. If you think about it, that means each kid was only allowed room for one mess or thing left out that entire week! This really kicked it into high gear, and we realized we were better off helping each other than letting everyone fend for themselves. Kaira would remind Elisa to clean up her lunch, or in some situations, we didn't even remind them, we just cleaned it up for them. I might put Magnus's leash away for Jackson or Sydney would put Kaira's violin away. We all knew that someone else had probably picked up one of our messes that week and so were more willing to clean up someone else's mess. We were all working together to make the house a cleaner place because we knew it would benefit us in the long run.

The first week we did this I think we got six, so everyone got a Hershey Kiss, but that left us more determined. We did it one more week, and we successfully got five, and we got to go see a movie!

Finding ways for the kids to take responsibility for themselves but not forget that they are on a team, is crucial and so beneficial in the long run.

JOURNAL BELOW:

WRITE WHAT YOU LEARNED, HOW IT WENT, AND WHAT
IMPACT IT'S HAVING ON YOUR FAMILY CULTURE.

13

KITCHEN BLITZ

WAYS TO IMPROVE

The kitchen is by far our messiest room. Not only because it's in the middle of the house, but also because everyone is so busy and going a million directions at once. We don't eat breakfast or lunch together often, so people are eating at different times and then no one takes responsibility to empty the dishwasher. More times than not, the dirty dishes pile up on the counter, Elisa bakes some cookies and thinks someone else might be happy to clean up after her since they get to eat freshly baked cookies. Then someone gets a box of cereal out and then decides they'd better leave it out "just in case" someone else might want to use it...you get the picture.

The kitchen is my zone, but zones only get done twice a week so what happens to the in-between times? Is Mom always responsible for it? Heck no. So we instated "kitchen blitzes." If you already have some sort of chore system down, like our zones, it might be useful to take a closer look at your messiest room and create some kind of blitz system in addition to the weekly times of cleaning.

It involves a whiteboard, of course, with everyone's name and a checkbox. Everyone, including Dad and Mom, needs to clean the kitchen for at least 15 minutes that week. If someone walked in the kitchen and the dishwasher was clean, the counters were dirty, and dishes needed to be done, they should show initiative to clean it on their own. Then they check their name off the list. The catch is that if someone leaves something out, Mom or Dad have the power to add another checkbox next to their name. And for every empty box, someone has left at the end of the week, they owe $5 to the fun jar. The idea of the fun jar is so we aren't just handing Dad and Mom 5 bucks, but it's going toward a future group experience. We still haven't spent the fun jar money, but it's building up to something big. We also light a kitchen candle, or as Dad has dubbed it, "The Candle of Blitz," after we're finished to signify the kitchen was just cleaned. We ran into a bit of a problem once when one kid finished a blitz, and another one came along, not knowing that a blitz was just completed, and decided to clean out the microwave or something that the first person hadn't done and then called it a blitz. OR the child who did the blitz would check off their name and then along would come a sibling and leave a mug on the counter. Mom would go in, see the cup and erase the person's check mark because they didn't do a good job. The candle just helped with misunderstandings like that.

Now in addition to kitchen blitz, everyone also has assigned dinner chores. I do the dishes, Jackson clears the table, Sydney wipes the table, Elisa sweeps, and Kaira sets the table.

So between our dinner chores, my zones, and the kitchen blitzes; our kitchen stays pretty clean.

JOURNAL BELOW:

WRITE WHAT YOU LEARNED, HOW IT WENT, AND WHAT IMPACT IT'S HAVING ON YOUR FAMILY CULTURE.

....

....

....

....

....

....

....

....

....

14

MENU PLANNING AND GROCERY SHOPPING

WAYS TO IMPROVE

Grocery shopping, meal planning, and cooking is no small task for any family, but our family of seven felt especially hard to manage at times (those families out there with 15 kids, not sure how they do it). But as I've said before, Mom is a planner and very resourceful, so this is another place her skills have blessed our family so much.

On Sunday (our first day of the work week) she would sit down with her cookbook or Pinterest board, planner, and grocery list to plan that week's meals. As we have gotten older, some of us cook dinner, so she consults the various cooks of the family about what they want to cook, and she develops the grocery list. The actual grocery shopping has been done many ways throughout the years. In the early years, it consisted mostly of her shopping with all us kids or trying to do it at a time where Dad could stay home with us. Currently, it consists of us paying someone to do it for us! Mostly because of how busy every member of our family is, not because we don't have capable children, who could drive themselves.

But we had a pretty good system worked out at one point that we thought might be helpful to some of you. I am a lot like my Mom. Super observant and organized, so when I was around 9 or 10 years old, Mom would make a list and take me to the grocery store. She would bring some work to do as she sat at the Kroger Starbucks while I did all the shopping. I would bring the cart back to Mom to evaluate before we checked out together. When I got a bit older, Mom would actually drop me off to do the whole thing by myself so that she could run other errands.

Another way we have done it is by giving the kids "missions." They love to feel independent, so if Mom had to take all us kids to the grocery store, she would group us into teams of two or three. Then she would give us a few items, that were found right next to each other, to go fetch and bring back to her. "I need you to go get sugar, flour, and vanilla then come meet me in the meat section." So we'd run off with our partner and sometimes it was successful, sometimes she would have to send us back to get a different brand, size, or flavor. What was nice about that method was it kept us busy, and Mom found everything actually went a lot faster.

Use the members of your team to accomplish tasks that occur regularly. If it's going to happen daily or weekly, it's worth it to find a life-giving system. Any way you can make the kids feel like they're on a team and improve the state of the team simultaneously...that's when you've hit the jackpot.

JOURNAL BELOW:

WRITE WHAT YOU LEARNED, HOW IT WENT, AND WHAT IMPACT IT'S HAVING ON YOUR FAMILY CULTURE.

TAKEAWAYS

Thanks for reading this book! We hope you enjoyed it and it has helped transform your family culture. Remember, this type of book wasn't meant to be read through in one sitting but instead meant to be almost a blueprint or manual of sorts to refer back to over time. And in the notes sections make marks and comments about how it goes, so next time you take a look through you can compare and see the difference!

Here are some broad overviews of some takeaways that you might forget if you read every single chapter and need a refresher!

- When you see a problem arise in your home culture, it is your job as the parents to fight against the chaos proactively. Get creative and even involve your kids in coming up with solutions.
- When implementing a new system, create a reward/consequence plan to help everyone catch on, stay motivated and train. Next, once it should be a habit, take away the reward so they only get a consequence if they don't adhere to the system. If they still resist, it's time for a heart-to-heart.
- Don't let a reward be for time with you. They will feel like they need to earn your attention instead of you giving it because you love them and are interested in what they are going through.
- When trying to be multi-generational, be sensitive to the resistance of the grandparents. Slowly enfold them as you see appropriate and make them feel honored above all else.
- When creating a team, competition between the siblings is never a good idea. We want them to celebrate each other's achievements, not fight to be first.
- When being on mission, show your kids what they're fighting for, how you going to work is part of the mission, and how they are a vital part of that mission.
- As parents, make sure you're doing everything within your power to stay on the same page, craft a home environment each other wants to be in, and work on your tools or systems together.
- Having a weekly meeting where the culture is discussed is really helpful for keeping everyone accountable and also checking in to see how everyone is doing.

Thanks so much for reading *31 Ways to Build your Family Team*. We sure love you guys and are rooting for your team!

KELSEY AND THE PRYOR FAMILY

Made in the USA
Las Vegas, NV
05 December 2021